save me

Gwendoline Meyers

Copyright © 2023 by Gwendoline Meyers

All rights reserved.

No portion of this book may be reproduced in any form without written permission from the publisher or author, except as permitted by U.S. copyright law.

contents

chapter one	1
chapter two	6
chapter three	11
chapter four	16
chapter five	24
chapter six	29
chapter seven	34
chapter eight	39
chapter nine	46
chapter ten	51
chapter eleven	57
chapter twelve	63
chapter thirteen	68

chapter fourteen	75
chapter fifteen	79
chapter sixteen	86
chapter seventeen	91
chapter eighteen	98
chapter nineteen	101
chapter twenty	105

chapter one

Ayden Grant

"you're worthless" "you're ugly" "you're a slut" "you're fat" "you're annoying" "you're stupid" "you're a waste of space" "why don't you just end your life already" "no one likes you" "you're weird"

Their words ran through my mind over and over again as I tossed and turned in my so called 'bed'. I reached for my phone and checked to see the time. The numbers "3:28" were written across the screen. Even if I went to sleep now I would only get 3 hours of sleep. Getting up at 6 in the morning everyday to go to school; a place I hate for many reasons. I put my phone back down on my nightstand. I rolled to the other side of my bed again trying to find a comfortable place and finally get some rest. Unfortunately for me as I closed my eyes all I could think about was those words. The ones I had been told so many times. I ask myself questions all the time. I tend to overthink everything in life.

What did I do to deserve this? Why does every bad thing happen to me? Does everything happen for reason? Will it ever get better?

But the one questions I ask myself everyday. The one question that could end all my pain and suffering in an instant.

What is the purpose in living anymore?

In the past few years my life went from average and me being happy to my worst nightmare.

On October 17th 2000 (age 17). I was born in the evening not exactly sure what time but around 7 or 8 o'clock. I was a healthy 8 pound baby boy. I was my moms first child and my dad's 3rd. He had two sons from a previous marriage that were ten and thirteen at the time. They named me Ayden grant. Just Ayden grant, I always thought it was kinda weird not having a middle name but I'm used to it now.

I had a pretty normal childhood until the summer of 8th grade. A few days after the Fourth of July my dad just left me and my mom and little brother. My older brothers were in their twenties at the time and lived on their own now.

My mom was probably the most affected by it. She would cry at night or when she was by herself. Whenever we saw her she always put a smile on her face and told us everything would be okay. I never had the connection with my dad like I had with my mom. Even before he left. He just wasn't as good as my mom was to put it harshly. Ever since then it's just been the three of us my mom, my brother Ryan, and me. We were all sad at first but got each other through it. I even think everybody was a little happier after my dad was gone.

The happiness didn't last long though. My mom had lost her job a few months before my dad left us. Now we were living in an apartment with no income. We moved to our grandmas house which was only a few minutes away from where we lived.

I started high school that year. It was decent. School work was kinda easy for me if I studied and payed attention in class. I had a few friends but I was no where near popular. I never wanted to be popular though. There was no point in being "friends" with people who would switch up on you in a minute. True friends are ones that stick by your side for everything.

9th grade year flew by pretty quickly. Nothing crazy really happened to me at least. I never had a relationship, got in a fight or been bullied by anyone yet. There weren't your typical bullies in high school that would shove you into lockers or beat you up in the hallway like in the movies. People would just talk about you behind your back or pretend to be your friend to get a good laugh.

10th grade flew by as well same friends and everything. Nothing to interesting had happened to me.

11th grade started and then everything went downhill from there. The school year started and I made a few new friends. I met this guy named Zack. He was attractive, an average nice, sweet guy who seemed pretty chill. I always knew I had liked boys so I had a crush on him of course. We started talking and our friendship led to a relationship. My first relationship I was 16 at the time. It was a year and a half ago. He was the first guy I ever loved. I was so infatuated with him. He was my everything. He was my first and only love to this day. One day he came up to me and told me he didn't love me and that he had been seeing someone else the whole time we had been together. My heart was shattered. I cried myself to sleep so many nights. I lost hope in everything. I felt numb. I didn't want to leave my bed. I hated my life.

I felt like I had no purpose in my life anymore.

I fell into a pretty bad depression where I hated everything in my life. I was always sad and never left my house except for school. This lasted a couple months. It's got a little bit better everyday and now I'm over him. However, him cheating on me has left me with a lot of problems. I have major trust issues, I'm always scared of people leaving me, I have anxiety. My family problems didn't help either.

A few months ago I found out my mom does drugs. And not like weed or alcohol even though I still wouldn't be happy with that. She does heroin. One of the worst drugs. She spends a lot of her money on it. I can't remember the last time she has bought me or my brother something nice with her money instead of spending it all on drugs.

That's how we've ended up here. We live in a pretty bad neighborhood now since we can't afford a nice house after we moved out of my grandmas. Most of the people around are involved in gangs, drugs, and other crimes. No surprise we live here then I guess. The house was pretty run down and looked gross from everywhere. I had a thin, dirty, old mattress that I slept on. Better than the cold floor I suppose.

"worthless" "ugly" "slut" "fat" "annoying" "stupid" "waste of space" "weird"

Those words were always in the back of my mind. They never left me alone especially at night. When I was the most vulnerable. Alone, in the middle of the night, sad and deep in my thoughts.

I checked my phone again to see what time it was.

"5:57" popped up on the screen. Great another sleepless night I thought to myself. Just what I needed at this moment.

Chapter Two

Ayden Grant

Pale with the slightest bit of tan. Blonde almost white hair, with a little wave. Shorter on the sides and longer on the top. Dark brown filled eyebrows with a slight arch. Black, Long, curly eyelashes with light blue iris that resembled the blue sky on a sunny day. A thin looking nose that led to beautiful light pink full lips and a sharp jawline. Slim body and 5'8" tall.

I wasn't that bad looking right?

"You're ugly" "you're fat". The words that always found a way to ruin even the slightest bit of happiness for me.

I walked back into my small bedroom and grabbed my backpack. I started walking to my bus stop. It was only a 5 minute walk but at 6 o'clock in the morning it was still pitch black out. Everyone was on their phones standing away from each other waiting for the bus to come. I usually sat by myself and hoped no one would take the seat next to me. I hated having to talk to people I didn't know. I was what you would call socially awkward. I couldn't hold a conversation for my life. I hated how shy and awkward I was at times. But I just couldn't help it. It's just who I am and who I will always be.

The quiet awkward boy. That's what people saw me as. It was true though. That's all I was. I didn't have very many friends. Only a couple that I wasn't even sure I could call my friends. I was a lonely person in general. I don't like being alone but I've gotten used to it over the years. I never really trusted anyone. Especially after him.

I stayed quiet in most of my classes doing my work and trying to draw as little attention to myself as possible. After 4th period I walked to lunch. It was on the other side of the school. As I walked to the cafeteria I saw people looking over at me. I was nothing special though. I ignored them and kept on walking. By the time I was in the lunch room everyone's eyes were on me.

Why was everyone looking at me?

A guy I didn't know walked up to me. He was a few inches taller so I had to look up to him.

"Wow can't believe you would do that" this mystery boy said.

"Do what?" I asked in complete confusion.

"Oh you know" he laughed. Some more people came over to watch what was going on. I was still confused about what he was talking about. People had started taking out their phones and recording the scene.

"Everyone's already seen the pictures by now. You don't have to act like you don't know. The whole school knows." The boy continued.

He pulled out his phone and held it in front of me. My mouth fell open and my eyes started to water. The picture he had pulled up on his phone was a picture of me. It wasn't just any picture of me tho. I was laying in bed with nothing on. I was completely naked.

It was a picture I had taken at the time I was dating Zach and sent it to him. He pressured me to do it even though I didn't like the idea of it. I trusted him so I agreed to send him nudes. He promised to never show anyone and that he would delete them yet they were on this guys phone and apparently everyone else's.

"I can't believe he would do that" "who would want to see that" "what a slut" "how disgusting" everyone was talking about me. They were all laughing or giving me disgusted looks while pointing my way.

I felt my breathing pick up and I started to sweat. I could feel my face becoming red from being the center of attention something I hated. I could feel my vision becoming blurry as I looked around at everyone still laughing at me. My hands started to shake. My eyes were stinging from the tears that were about to fall any second.

I turned around and ran as fast as I could out of the cafeteria. I ran inside the closet building looking for a bathroom. I went into the first stall and locked the door. I turned around and just started crying. My face was completely red by now and covered in tears. I tried to calm myself down but all I could think about was the pictures and how disgusting I was. I was a slut. Everyone at school at seen my naked body. Each time I thought about one of their words I started crying harder and harder. I had a horrible headache now. Crying always gave me headaches.

I grabbed some toilet paper and started to wipe my eyes. I tried breathing slow in a way to calm myself down. I sat in the bathroom for a few more minutes just doing this. I unlocked the stall and walked to the sink. I looked at myself in the mirror. My face was a little pink still as well as my eyes from the tears. I splashed my face with cold water. It helped cool my face down a little and made me feel somewhat better.

I washed my hands and walked out of the bathroom. There was only a couple minutes of lunch left so I decided to start walking to my fifth period. I kept my head down avoiding all the stares from the other students. I just wanted this day to be over already.

I tried to keep to myself and ignore the stares I was getting in my classes. It wasn't easy. I could feel their eyes watching me like I was some kind of science experiment. I hated it. I hated being in the spotlight. Thankfully the day would be over soon and I could go home.

The bus ride was the same as in my classes; hateful looks and laughter directed at me.

They were laughing at me not with me.

Chapter Three

Ayden Grant

The deep red trickled down my fair looking skin. The liquid dripped onto the tile floor joining the puddle of blood that was already there. Cutting gave me control. I was in control of my own pain.

I had 3 cuts horizontally along my left arm. I didn't know how deep they are. I cut myself with a knife we had in the kitchen. I was sitting on my bathroom floor alone. I had no idea what time it was or how long I had been in here.

What is the purpose in living anymore?

A question I had been asking myself more often. It's been 3 days since "the incident" as I called it. The day at school where everyone saw the picture. I still didn't even know how that picture had gotten around to everyone. It's been over a year since we broke up so why would Zack send it now? We hadn't been in each other's life for months. Why did he still even have the picture?

I looked down and saw my wrist was cover in blood from the cuts. I hadn't cleaned them yet. They had stopped bleeding after a few minutes. I got up and washed off my wrists. The warm water stung a little but it wasn't that bad. I grabbed some toilet paper and cleaned the blood off the floor.

I decided to go on a walk. Walking gave me time to think about life. It was Friday night. Most teens would be at parties or with their friends, but not me. I had no friends and I was too socially awkward to go to a party. I was a weird teenager. Being a teen is supposed to be one of the best times of your life. This is one of the worst times of my life.

I walked down my street for about 10 minutes. There was a park at the end of it that a lot of people went too. It had a playground for kids, a lake for fishing and a couple basketball courts. I come down here a lot to be alone and reflect.

There were guys playing basketball. Little kids on the swings. A few families throwing bread to the ducks. The park was pretty lively today.

I wonder where I'll be in 5 years from now. What kind of job I would have? Where I would live? Would I even be alive? I thought about the future often. I tend to overthink a lot of situations. I was always worried about what was going to happen next in my life.

Would I ever be truly happy again? What is happiness? Is happiness just our imaginations? I'm overthinking once again.

I found a bench and sat down for a little while. I started at the people around the park. I wonder what their lives were like. It's crazy how we judge people based on the way they look and think we can know everything about them.

I don't remember exactly how much time I spent at the park that day observing people and thinking about what their lives are like. It was fascinating to me to think you could know someone, so well yet know barely anything at the same time.

The sun had started to go down, so I decided I should be heading home. Not like my mom would care she was probably high or out buying some kind of drug to use later tonight.

I wonder why she did that. I don't think anybody just decides that they wanna do heroin. Something has to happen to them that they want to forget so the use drugs to numb their pain.

I guess it was kinda like when I cut myself. It was a way for me to control the pain. But drugs aren't good for you, they can kill you.

But cutting yourself wasn't healthy either. There is a better way to deal with pain. I just don't know how to.

I came home to see my mom wasn't there, but I'm not really surprised. My brother was in his room playing on his xbox, of course. The kid was obsessed with it. It was a pretty old version but hey it still worked. And besides we didn't have the money to buy a new one.

I walked in his room and sat on his bed. He didn't bother turning around, he was too engrossed in the video game he was playing.

"Hey Ryan" I said trying to get his attention. He finally turned around.

"I thought you went for a walk?" he asked.

"Yeah, I did. Just got back and thought we could talk for a little bit." I told him.

He turned around fully facing me and completely forgetting the video game.

"Yeah what's up?" he asked.

"I feel like we should hangout more. Spend more time together. I miss it." It was true. We hadn't spent as much time together in the past few years. We grew up really close as little kids but we had just drifted apart over the past few years.

"I miss you too Ayden. I miss the fun times we had as kids. All the games we would play and accuse each other of cheating. Or when we would do things just to annoy the other" he laughed thinking about our childhood.

"Yeah we used to be really close." I reminded him.

"Wanna play some games. I have a few and I could teach you how to play them." He offered.

"Give me a controller and I'll beat you at anything" I challenged him. I knew I couldn't. I was horrible at video games but it was fun to mess with my brother.

"Oh you're on" he said throwing me the controller.

We played a few different games that night. Mostly me losing while Ryan completely destroyed me. Laughing every time I would get confused or not know how to play.

I felt like I had a brother again. I felt this feeling I hadn't felt in awhile. I was feeling happiness.

Chapter Four

Ayden Grant

"I love you both so much. I will miss you guys. I love you." Our mom told us while hugging me and my little brother. She was leaving. She needed this though. She needed to get help.

My mom was going to a rehab center for drug addicts. I was glad that she was getting the help she needed but also sad that I wouldn't get to see her. I loved my mom more than anything in the world. She was the most important person to me.

A cop had found her on the sidewalk passed out. He brought her back home. He thought she should go to a rehab center instead of jail time. She could get the help she needs and become clean there. It was best for her.

The cop that had found our mom was also the school's resource officer. I didn't know him that well but had seen around the school a few times. He seemed like a nice guy.

I was 17 turning 18 in just 3 months. I was close to being an adult but I couldn't live on my own but they wouldn't bother putting me in the foster care system. My brother on the other hand was 12. He still had years before he would be on his own. I wasn't sure where we were going to go or what would happen next. I didn't wanna be separated from my brother but I knew it was a possibility. We didn't have any relatives either that could take care of us. I can't remember any of them. We hadn't seen them since we were kids.

When things were good.

Even if I did turn 18 in a few months I couldn't take care of myself and him. For one I didn't have much money. I had a job but it didn't pay enough to pay for rent, water, electricity, food and other basic necessities.

I had a lot of unanswered questions. I hated the unknown. It scared me not knowing what was going to happen. I liked to be in control of my life.

We were all still standing in the room. The officer turned to me and said "we're going to take your mother to get help. This is what's best for her well being and both of yours. We will find a place for both of you to live temporarily since your mother will not be able to take care of you."

Another officer had taken my mom after saying our goodbyes and to this rehab place that I didn't know the name of.

The school resource officer, I don't remember what his first name was but I knew his last name was Reese. He had a gold little badge that had Officer Reese embedded into it.

"Come on. I'll take you back to the station and will figure out a living situation for now." He told us reassuringly.

We both followed him out of the house and to his cop car. I had never been a cop car before. It looked kinda cool. I wonder what kind of people had been in the back of this car for. Why do people commit crimes?

Officer Reese started driving back to the police station. It wasn't too far from our house actually. It was right next to the elementary school me and my brother attended when we were kids.

We got out of the car and followed officer Reese into the station. It wasn't what I assumed it to be like. There was a lady behind the desk, a receptionist. We walked past her into a hallway that had different rooms marked with the different names of the cops that worked here, I'm assuming. We walked into the one that had sheriff's office written on it. Inside the room was a large dark brown desk with a laptop, some papers, a cup holder with pens. Just typical office supplies I suppose. There were a few chairs in front of the desk. While the man behind the desk I'm presuming as the sheriff, had put down the paper he had been holding as we walked in.

Me and my brother both sat down in the chairs leaving one for officer Reese.

"Their mother is in a rehab facility for the next few months. They don't have any relatives to take care of them for the time being. Ayden will be turning. 18 In a few months so putting him in foster care would be pointless. I also do not want to separate the both of them from each other." The officer explained.

The sheriff looked over at us not saying anything, just thinking for a moment.

"They're mother would only be gone temporarily, and would come back soon so I don't think foster care is really an option." The sheriff replied.

"You know me and my wife have taken kids in before temporarily, in situations like this. I wouldn't mind doing it again. I would just have to talk to her about it." Officer Reese brought up an idea. This helped sooth my thoughts. Me and my brother would still be together. We would be safe. Everything would be okay.

The sheriff looked replied with "Go home and talk to you're wife about it and if you still want to go through with it then, the living arrangements should be fine."

Officer Reese nodded at him and stood up. He motioned for us to follow him out. He started explaining to us that we might be living with his family temporarily, if the idea was okay with his wife. He reassured us that she would probably be okay with the idea and that we would be staying there for the next few months. Me and my brother were both fine with the idea.

When we got to his house he lead us into a living room area with a few couches and chairs, a big t.v. and family pictures hung up around on the walls. The house looked nice from the outside and the inside or at least what I had seen so far. He told us we could watch t.v. while he had a talk with his wife. He showed us how to use the remote and walked into to a dining room area.

"Do you think everything will be okay?" Ryan asked bringing me out of my thoughts.

I looked over at him he seemed a little worried. "Yeah, were in a cops house, nothing bad happens here" I laughed a little thinking about illegal activities in a cops house. Ryan seemed reassured with my answer and turned back to the t.v. We continued to watch whatever show was on until we heard officer Reese and his wife come out from the kitchen.

"We've decided that it would be best for the both of you to stay here for now." Officer Reese said.

"We have 1 spare bedroom and our other son has a room that we could put another bed in." His wife added in.

"Thank you both so much for letting us stay here" I said. I really appreciated them letting me and my brother, practically strangers to them, into their house and letting us live here.

"You don't have to thank us. We love to help people. Now come on let's get you both settled in." She gestured for us to follow her. She led us down a hallway stopping at a room.

She opened the door. The walls were white with nothing hung up making them looking really plain. There was a bed in the corner of the room with a blue and white bed set. A brown dresser in front of it a t.v. sitting on top. There were two white closet doors on the other side. It was an average size room. Big enough for one, even two people.

"This will be your room Ryan. Feel free to make yourself at home." She told him. My brother walked in and looked around observing his new room.

"Thank you" he said to her. She just nodded and said she was going to show me my room.

We kept walking down a hallway. At the end of the hallway was a bathroom. Then there were two doors facing each other. She explained the one on the left was her and her husbands. The one on the right was her sons room which I would be sharing with.

"My son is 18 just a year older than you. I believe you both go to the same high school if I'm right. You two are closer in age so I think it will be better if you two shared a room instead. He's out with some of his friends right now but he should be back within a few hours" she explained to me.

Inside the room the walls were white, a few posters of "hot" almost naked girls were hung up. There was a bed in the center of the room with a nightstand next to it. There was a full length mirror next to the closet door. Along with a dresser and a t.v. sitting on it. I would say it was little bit bigger than the previous room but not huge.

I thanked her and walked in just looking around.

"I know you don't have a bed yet but we can go out tonight and get a frame and some new sheets. We have an extra mattress in storage. For the meantime make yourself at home. Dinner will be done in an hour or so." She explained.

"I'm very grateful for everything you're doing for me and my brother" I thanked her again. She gave me a hug and reassured me that she was glad to be helping us.

"Oh and by the way I forget to tell you my name is Stacey and my husbands name is Sean. Just call us by our first names. Ms. Reese makes me feel old." She laughed out. I nodded and she walked out to start making dinner.

I sat in bean bag chair that had been on the floor and started thinking about life. Something I did quite often.

Was I getting a fresh start in life?

Chapter Five

Cameron Reese

"Bro did you see that picture" my friend Luke asked me.

"Who hasn't see that picture yet?" I laughed.

Everyone had seen the picture of Ayden Grant naked. There were tons of rumors going around about him. I didn't know who he was until the picture. I don't think anybody knew about him till then.

The rumor was Ayden Grant was desperate. He wanted his ex boyfriend back "Zack" was his name I think, so he sent him nudes. Who would do that?

"Everybody's been talking about it" Luke replied. I mean who wouldn't be right?

"Yeah, it's disgusting that someone would do that." I said. Ayden Grant was basically a slut. Showing off his body to try and be with someone.

"I gotta go home, mom will be mad if I miss dinner. Not like it matters though. Her cooking is bad." I said to Luke. We both went our separate ways to our cars.

Car rides was were I thought about life. I didn't like my mom or dad for that matter. They were annoying. My dad was a cop. My mom worked in some office job. Nothing special really.

I had money, friends, I was pretty popular at my school, I had good looks. I had short brown hair a few inches long on the top and closely shaved on the sides. It was a pretty popular style nowadays. I had medium brown eyebrows that were just kinda straight. I had very light green eyes that I got complimented on all the time. I had a few freckles but not a lot to really notice unless you were up close to my face. I had light pinkish full lips with a sharp jawline. I was pretty tall around 6'3" something I inherited from my dad. I had a nice body as well. I worked out a few times a week and kept it in shape.

I wasn't the best kid. I didn't like my parents. I've done a lot of different drugs in the past. I still smoke weed every now and then with my friends or when I'm by myself. I drink alcohol but it's not as good as weed is to me. It was kinda hard to smoke when your dad's a cop.

I walked in my house and went straight to my bedroom. I put my keys on my dresser and walked back out. I walked into the dining room and saw my parents but with two strangers. One boy looked to be in middle school and the other looked around my age.

"Hi honey, I want you to meet Ryan" she gestured to the younger boy and "Ayden" she gestured to the boy who looked to be my age.

Ayden. Ayden Grant. The boy everyone at school was talking about. Was in my house. Eating dinner with my parents.

"They're going to be staying with us for the next few months" my mom continued. I was used to my parents fostering kids temporarily. It was nice not being alone all the time I actually enjoyed it but this was different.

This was Ayden Grant. The school whore. The one that everyone had seen naked in a photo.

I couldn't believe my parents were allowing that into the house. He was disgusting.

I walked over to the table and sat down. We had dinner, my mom was actually pretty good at cooking but I was to stubborn to say something nice about my parents.

During dinner I was thinking if i should pretend to be friends with him or just act how I really feel whenever my parents weren't around. I figured I could act friendly in front of my parents but when we were alone or at school I could do and say whatever I wanted to him. I didn't feel bad about it at all. In my opinion he deserved it. He practically asked for it.

"Oh and by the way, Cameron you will be sharing your room with Ayden from now on. We've already moved another mattress into their. Me and your father are going shopping for a bed set." My mom explained. Oh you gotta be kidding me. They thought I was gonna share a room with that. They've got to be out of their minds now.

"Great" I said trying to conceal my anger and forcing out a smile. I guess this meant more alone time to mess with him. Oh I can't wait.

Dinner was soon over and both my parents left to go shopping. Me and Ayden were both in my room on our own beds. I sat up and looked over at him. He looked really deep in thought.

"So you're that desperate huh?" I asked messing with him. He looked over at me with a confused expression.

"What are you talking about?" He asked. So he's trying to act like he doesn't know what he did.

"Everybody knows. Wait till my parents here about this. They would kick you out immediately. You know child pornography is very illegal. You could be put in jail for awhile." I said trying to scare him. I don't think I would tell my parents. That would ruin all the fun I could have messing with Ayden. Speaking of him, he looked terrified like he had just seen a ghost.

"I was pressured into it. I didn't wanna do it but I did." He said trying to make it seem like he hadn't done anything and that he was innocent, yet he was far from that.

"You should drop this little innocent act you have going on. You were desperate. So you sent Zack that pic to try and get him back. You're just a whore Ayden. Who shows off their naked body for attention. That's the only reason the whole school is talking about you. Oh If you try and tell anyone about this living arrangement" I pointed between the both of us. "It's not going to end well for you to put it simply" I finished my little rant.

He just sat there not saying a word after. His eyes were watering and he was about to cry. How pathetic I thought. Who could possibly like that?

Chapter Six

Ayden Grant

I was disgusting. Everyone thought so. It was true though. Even if I didn't send the picture willingly I still did it and now I have to deal with the consequences of it. This picture was ruining my life. I had gone from the unknown boy to the school whore. That's what everyone thought I was.

I was laying in my bed across from Cameron. He had told me everything about the rumors and called me names. I was crying and my body was shaking a little. I didn't want it to be too noticeable though. I had already been embarrassed enough in front of him and on the first day we met. I felt worthless. I felt disgusted with myself. I felt like I was a slut. I felt humiliated. Mostly I felt used. I hated this feeling. I hated how weak I was. I would cry at names that shouldn't hurt me or rumors that weren't even true. But they really did hurt. I tried to ignore it but I just couldn't. It was too hard for me. To think everyone thought these rumors were true hurt me so bad.

I continued crying in my bed. I was facing against the wall so Cameron couldn't see me but I'm sure he could hear me. I wasn't really that quiet.

"Are you seriously crying?" he laughed out. "Wow, pathetic" He continued.

His words just made me cry harder. Hearing them out loud made it worse. I rolled over so I was on the other side of my bed, facing him. I stood up and walked out of the room. He just watched me not saying anything else to me. I walked down the hallway to the bathroom. I locked the door behind me. I grabbed some tissues drying up my face. I looked in the mirror. My face was bright shade of pink as well as my eyes. My face was a little wet from my tears. I looked weak. He was right.

I looked around on the counters searching for a pill bottle. I opened it up and dumped them out on the counter. I wonder how many of these it would take to overdose on. 20, 30, more? I wanted to do it so badly. I wanted to end my pain. I picked up a handful of them. I don't know how many I was holding.

Just do it already. Nobody cares. You won't be missed.

I had no one that loved me. I had no friends. I was a slut. I was worthless. I had no reason to live. I was a mistake. I never should have been born.

I took the pills I was holding. There were still some on the counter but I just left them there. I had taken around 15 or something I wasn't really sure.

I took off my clothes and got in the shower. The water felt so warm. Warm water was soothing to me. It helped me calm down. I felt drowsy. I was leaning against the wall with my eyes half opened. Maybe those pills were sleeping pills? I didn't read the label so I had no idea. My eyes were slowly closing. I tried so hard to keep them open but I couldn't.

I was half asleep when I heard a loud crashing noise. I felt cold and wet. I couldn't open my eyes though. I was still so tired.

"What the fuck?! Are you kidding me?" I heard someone say.

I felt something touching me but I didn't really care. I was so tired right now. Whatever was touching me now felt warm instead of the cold.

"I can't believe he did this. What's wrong with him?" I heard more mumbling.

I felt someone shaking my body in an attempt to wake me up. My eyes refused to open. I hadn't slept long enough to be woken up.

"Wake the fuck up already" the voice yelled at me while shaking me harder.

My eyes finally opened. I looked up and saw Cameron over me practically glaring at me.

"You were laying on the bathroom floor." He explained.

I had a bad headache, did I hit my head? I felt cold too.

"I heard a crashing noise and the water had been on for awhile. So I thought you fell or something." He continued.

Cameron walked to the other side of the room and sat on the edge of his bed. He had some kind of game controller in his hand and his headphones on.

"I'm back" he said to whoever he was talking too.

I looked down at myself. I had a towel wrapped around my hips. My body had little droplets of water still. My hair was wet too.

I was in the shower naked. Cameron saw me naked. And wrapped my body in a towel.

Cameron Reese saw me naked. Well I mean he had already seen the picture but this was in real life.

Oh my. I thought to myself. I didn't have a nice body. I didn't have abs or big muscles like other guys. I was average or even below average.

I shouldn't care about what he thinks of me.

But I do.

I got up and looked through my bag for new clothes to put on. I walked back into the bathroom and got dressed.

Does he know I took the pills? Does he even care?

I mean, he didn't say anything about it if he did notice. I wish they would have worked. I looked at myself in the mirror and noticed my jaw was red like I had been punched or hurt.

I looked down to the counter to see the pills still lying there.

baby aspirin low dosage

No wonder it didn't work. You need about four baby aspirin to equal one normal size pill. so i had only taken about 3 or 4 pills. Nothing enough to actually hurt me.

I failed this time. Like always

chapter seven

Ayden Grant

Saturday morning. Still alive. It's been one day at my new home. I won't be doing anything today with friends. Not like I have any.

Cameron wasn't in his room so I assumed he was with his friends or something. He probably has a social life, unlike me.

1:23

Omg. I had slept in till 1 o'clock. I usually only sleep till about ten. Eleven at the latest. I can't remember the last time I slept in this late.

I headed downstairs to see Mrs. Reese cooking lunch. It smelled so good.

"Good afternoon, honey" she chirped. I asked what she was making. Spaghetti, one of my favorite foods. I haven't actually had in awhile.

"It smells delicious" I told her. I loved the smell of garlic. Who doesn't?

We ate lunch and the rest of the day went by pretty boring. I didn't do anything really.

On Sunday I did the same thing. Just sit around the house. Think about life. Something I do too much.

Monday morning. I hated Monday's. I'm pretty sure everyone does. I walked to school. It only took about 10 minutes. At least I didn't have to ride the bus anymore and we were closer to the school.

"Look who showed up. The school whore. Ayden Grant" I think his name was Luke. I didn't really know many peoples name. I didn't like talking to people.

"Not gonna say anything, huh?" Luke asked. Was I really a slut? I didn't send that picture willingly. I knew it was a bad idea, I shouldn't have send it in the first place. It was so stupid.

"Freak!" He yelled and pushed me into the lockers. Which hurt very much. I groaned in pain, still not replying to him.

I saw a group of people circling around looking to watch a fight. Some had their phones out recording.

"I didn't do anything" I whispered, desperately trying to defend myself. I really hadn't. I knew no one would believe me though. Everyone was against my side.

"What was that, freak?" Luke asked.

"I said I didn't do anything" I spoke louder almost yelling but not quite. I saw his face turn into anger.

I saw him raise his hand and I knew he was about to hit me.

"Don't raise your voice at me, like that" he spoke with anger in his voice.

Luke punched me in my face. I immediately felt my jaw explode with pain. I groaned loudly from the pain in my face.

"You deserve that. Slut. Nobody wants you. Just kill yourself already" he said to me. All the people around laughing and still recording.

I deserved to die. I didn't even wanna be alive. Nobody liked me. I didn't even like myself.

I looked around and saw everyone staring and laughing. I started breathing quickly and felt my face get red from embarrassment. I felt like I was having a panic attack. My eyes started watering and I felt a few tears slip out.

"Awe look. The freak is crying how pathetic! What a-" Luke started but was cut off when someone yelled his name.

"Luke. What are you doing?" The voice sounded familiar but I wasn't sure who it was. I didn't look up. I was so embarrassed right now. The whole school saw me get punched and cry.

"Messing with the freak of the school" Luke replied.

"Leave him alone. Class is about to start anyways" the guy replied. "Come on. Go to class now" he yelled at the people still recording.

I heard the footsteps and whispers of people shuffling away, hopefully with Luke too.

"I'll meet you in class. I gotta do something first" I heard the mystery guys voice say. It sounded so familiar I just couldn't place a name to it though.

I heard footsteps get louder and saw the shoes were now in front of mine. I finally looked up to see who it was.

Cameron. Cameron Reese. The guy I was now living with. Him.

He looked at me with this look in his eyes but I couldn't decipher what it was.

"Are you okay? Did he touch you? Did he hurt you? What did he say?" Cameron asked me. I still had tears in my eyes.

I looked down and cried harder. He pulled me into a hug. He had his arms wrapped around me. "It's okay. It's okay." He repeated to me.

"Don't listen to him. Or any of them. You're not a freak. You're not a slut. You're not a whore. You matter and you're important" he told me.

Why was he telling me this? He didn't even know me. I don't even he likes me. Nobody does.

I saw him raise his hand and I flinched as a natural response. He sighed and wiped my tears away saying "I'm not gonna punch you".

I don't understand why he was being kind to me. I really don't.

"Let's go to class. You don't wanna be late" Cameron said. We both walked out separate ways to our classes.

That was weird I thought. Cameron Reese was nice? He wasn't an asshole like the other day. What is happening?

I pondered that thought for the rest of the day.

Chapter Eight

Cameron Reese

I don't know why I helped him. He looked so sad. I hate that look on his face. He's too beautiful to be sad.

Woahhh waitt.

I didn't just think Ayden Grant is beautiful. Nope not at all. Boys aren't beautiful. Especially a whore like him.

But was he? What if he didn't send the picture? I mean his face was clearly in the picture. So obviously he sent it. But ugh. I don't even know.

I couldn't watch Luke hurt him. Even though I wanted to just a few days ago. When I saw him sitting at the kitchen table with my parents. After I had just seen the picture of him. And to find out he was living with me.

Why did I defend him?

I told him he wasn't a whore or slut. But he is. I comforted him. But I didn't like him. I wanted him to feel better. But I wanted to hurt him. I didn't want Luke to hurt him but I did.

But did I?

Did he even deserve any of this? What if the pic was just a mistake. Even if it wasn't, it's not like nobody in high school hasn't ever sent a nude before.

The only difference was the whole school saw his. Others were private and only meant for that one person.

Did he even send the picture to get his ex, Zach, to get him back? Was it all just a lie? I was so confused with this whole situation. I didn't know who to believe.

I walked into my first period. Late of course because of the incident with Ayden.

School flew by pretty quickly. Surprisingly for a Monday. Usually Monday's felt like they lasted forever.

I was thinking about Ayden for a majority of the day. I remember the words I said to him the first day we met, which was only a few days ago.

You're just a whore Ayden. Who shows off their naked body for attention.

I wasn't sure if I meant those words or not. I didn't know if I wanted to take them back now or not.

1:33 a.m.

I turned over in my bed. I couldn't sleep. I had too much on my mind from the day. I looked over too see Ayden sleeping. The room was dark but the moonlight shone through the window.

He looked so peaceful. Unlike earlier today. His face was a little red still from that punch. His hair was messy and his lips were slightly parted.

He looked cute.

No. No. No. He didn't look cute. Ayden didn't look cute sleeping. Boys aren't cute. Especially Ayden. Not at all.

Ding. I looked down at my phone and didn't see a message. That's weird I thought. I heard the notification but hadn't received one.

Ding. I heard it again. It's not me. I know I heard a sound.

I looked up and saw Ayden's phone light up. Someone was texting him. I looked at my phone 1:44 a.m.

Who the fuck was texting him this late? I wanted to see who it was, but that's an invasion of privacy. Right?

Ding. The curiosity was killing me. They do say curiosity killed the cat. Guess I was the cat in this situation.

I wouldn't look at his messages. Just turn off the phone, so he wouldn't wake up.

I'm Cameron Reese. Since when do i care if I invade someone's privacy? Especially s Ayden's? And secondly, why do I care if he gets woken up.

I got up and grabbed his phone off the nightstand. As I picked it up it went off again. Lighting up the screen.

Four messages from four random numbers.

1:37 a.m. "kill yourself whore"1:39 a.m. "just die. nobody likes you"1:44 a.m. "slut. whore. desperate."1:47 a.m. "why don't you do the world a favor and end your life. Obviously nobody fucking likes you. You're never gonna find someone who will love a whore like you."

I gripped the phone harder. Who the fuck was sending these messages. It wasn't just one person. It was four different people. Someone leaked his number and now people were sending him death threats.

I was angry. I quickly opened the iMessage app and blocked all four numbers and then deleted them. I didn't want Ayden to see that. He didn't deserve it. No one deserves to be treated this way.

He made one little mistake. And everyone was acting like it's the worst thing a person has done.

I put his phone down and walked out of the room. I was mad. I knew he was probably going to get more texts and I couldn't delete them all.

I paced back and forth in the hallway. I didn't know what to do. I didn't know how to stop this. I didn't like Ayden. Obviously. But sending death threats was too far. He shouldn't have to deal with this.

I walked into the bathroom and gripped the counter until my knuckles turned white. I was seething. I couldn't stop myself from being so angry.

I turned and punched the closet thing to me. A small round mirror. Probably not the smartest idea. Since the glass broke and now my hand was bleeding but I didn't even care at the moment. I couldn't even feel the pain because I was so mad at the moment.

The sound of the mirror breaking was loud enough that it apparently woke Ayden up. He stumbled into the bathroom and saw me standing there with my hand bleeding.

He still looked half asleep. His hair was sticking up and his eyes were still half closed. He looked adorable.

No. He didn't. I told myself.

"What happened?" Ayden asked. His voice was slightly deeper than usual. It was sexy. No it wasn't.

"Umm I-I uh" I fumbled over my words. What the fuck is wrong with me. I never stutter or get nervous.

Ayden just stared at me and stared walking closer. He picked up my hand and examined it closely.

His hands felt so warm and soft. I wonder if he uses lotion. What the fuck am I thinking.

"You should probably wash that" he suggested, dropping my hand. He turned around and walked out of the bathroom and back to the room I'm assuming.

I washed my hand and tried it. I grabbed a bandage and wrapped it up.

I walked back to my room and saw Ayden sitting on his phone on his bed.

Oh shit. Did somebody else text him. He stared at his phone and then laughed.

Well I guess it's not a text from one of those people. But who's texting him this late and making him laugh.

Nobody should be texting Ayden this late. Their keeping him awake and making him laugh.

He put his phone down and laid down in his bed and turned over. I did the same and tried to go back to sleep. Today's been an interesting Monday I thought to myself.

chapter nine

Ayden Grant

Tuesday was less eventful than Monday. I got some dirty looks and comments from people. I didn't have any more encounters with Luke luckily. Wednesday was pretty much the same as Tuesday.

Thursday morning. I woke up early today. At 5:30. I tried going back to sleep but I couldn't fall back asleep so I got up and got dressed and ready for school.

I made some cereal and ate it quickly getting ready to leave for school. Today was extra cold out. I didn't realize that until I stepped outside.

I ran back inside and went upstairs to look for a jacket. I opened the bedroom door and ran in. I stopped when I saw Cameron turned around going through his closet. He was only wearing boxers.

He had a nice body. His back was muscular but not the unattractive kind. His arms flexed when he reached for his shirt.

Cameron had a sexy body. That was undeniable. I realized I had been staring for a minute and quickly walked over to the side of my bed and searched for jacket.

I found one and made my way downstairs and out of the house to school. School was okay. Nothing bad happened. Nothing good happened. It was just kinda average. People had been talking less about the whole picture incident.

Which I was very thankful for. I felt like it would never stop. I still got comments and looks but not nearly as bad as Monday and Tuesday.

This was high school. They moved on quickly to the next stupid drama of the week.

Today and Friday went by pretty fast. It was the weekend. Not like I would be doing anything special. I never do.

I don't like talking to people. Especially new people. I don't like social interaction is how I like to put it.

I'm an introverted person. I haven't ever been to a party, done drugs, anything illegal. I kinda had a boring life. I didn't do much.

I got home and went upstairs to the bedroom Cameron and I shared. Cameron was sitting on his bed playing his video games. He looked over at me for a second then looked back to his game.

"Fuck" he said to whoever he was talking too. "I died already. Yeah I gotta go I'll be back on later" he said.

"Let's talk" he said looking over at me and putting his controller down.

"About what?" I asked. I didn't know what he wanna talk about.

"Did you send that picture?" He asked. Again.

"No" I sighed. "I told you already I didn't do it willingly. It was so stupid and a dumb mistake" I replied.

"Why did you do it then?" He asked me.

Why did I do it? Why was I trying to make Zack happy. He never sent me anything back. But I trusted him. He broke that trust.

"Idk" I replied honestly. I don't know why.

"I believe you". I looked up shocked that someone believed me. Someone was on my side for once. But not just anybody. Cameron Reese. Out of all people.

"Um, thanks.." I wasn't sure how to reply. I wasn't expecting him to ever think I was telling the truth. I didn't think anybody would ever believe me.

Cameron stood up and walked over to the side of the room where my bed was. Which I was sitting on. He looked down at me and didn't say anything.

"What are you doing?" I asked nervously. He was standing above me not saying anything.

He grabbed my arm and examined it. He looked at my wrist and rubbed his thumb over them. Over my scars from my self inflicted cuts.

He looked up at me with a look of sadness in his eyes. How did he even notice those? They're so small and barley noticeable.

"Why?" Is all he said, referring to my wrists.

"It helps me deal with the pain" I answered honestly.

"There's other ways" he said. I knew there were other ways to deal with pain. I didn't know how to though. I wanted a quick solution to my problem and that was the solution. It was my only way to be in control.

Cameron let go of my wrists and sighed. He walked back over to his bed and went on his phone and then back to his video game.

I got my backpack and started doing some homework. I was in algebra II. It was difficult and I didn't understand a lot of the time. I always struggled in math.

I finished all of my school work after a few hours. I was so tired from school and all the drama in my life recently.

6:48 p.m.

I stood up and stretched my arms and legs. I let out a sigh and walked to the bathroom to take a bath.

I love baths. They're so relaxing and lovely. I stayed in there for an hour or so. I was so tired, I just wanted to go to sleep already.

I walked back to the bedroom in a just a towel. Cameron immediately looked over at me. He stared at me the whole time as I went through my clothes. I grabbed just a pair of boxers to sleep in.

I looked over at him and he turned back around to his video game. "Yeah, sorry got distracted" he said.

I put on my underwear and climbed into bed. I pulled my blanket over myself and closed my eyes. Life wasn't bad? I thought to myself.

I fell asleep soon after laying down.

Chapter Ten

Cameron Reese

He walked in and he only had a towel wrapped around his waist. Ayden walked over to his bed looking through his clothes and I couldn't help but stare at him.

His wasn't extremely muscular but he had a nice body. He turned around and looked at me. I turned back around to my game. I had died and didn't even notice because I was looking at Ayden.

I looked back at him and he was wearing just boxers. Fuck. He had a nice ass.

What the fuck am I thinking. Boys aren't cute. Boys don't have nice asses. But Ayden does.

"I'm gonna go" I told my friends on my PlayStation. I put my controller up and looked at my phone.

11:56 p.m.

I needed some weed. I went over to my closet and pulled out some I had already rolled up. I grabbed my lighter and went over to my bed. I opened my window up to let the smell out.

After 40 minutes I was so high. I started getting horny. This usually happens when I get high. I grabbed my phone and searched for porn to watch.

I opened the first tab and started watching two girls making out. I kept watching it for about 10 minutes but nothing was happening. I wasn't getting turned on at all.

I wasn't even slightly hard yet. Usually by now I would be so turned on yet I felt nothing.

I scrolled down the page and found a video of two guys. I hesitated before clicking on it and opening it.

I started watching the video. It started off with two guys making out. Then one getting on his knees and sucking off the other one. I felt my dick get hard immediately. I was shocked and confused.

Was I gay? Straight? Bisexual? I didn't even know at this point. I didn't care right now. I just wanted to feel good and enjoy this moment.

I reached into my pants and pulled out my dick. The guy was still giving the other a blow job. He was moaning and calling him daddy. I got even harder if that was possible. I started stroking my dick. It felt so good. It felt better than any other time I had masturbated.

The two guys on the video started fucking and I felt my myself getting hotter. I was so horny at the moment that I couldn't even think about anything else. I looked over and saw Ayden had the blanket only covering his lower legs and exposing his ass but still covered with his boxers. It looked so soft and fuckable.

I kept staring at him while touching myself. I felt like I was about to cum any second. Then I remembered the picture. I knew it was wrong and I shouldn't have done it.

I opened up my photo album on my phone and scrolled through my pictures until I found the pic of Ayden. The one where he was naked and touching himself. I looked at the picture until I came which only took a few seconds. It was one of the best orgasms I ever had. There was so much of my cum all over my chest. I laid in bed and just breathed for a minute. I can't believe I just did that.

I got up and went to the bathroom cleaning off my chest. I went back to my room and walked over to Ayden. I pulled his blanket back over his chest to keep him warm.

I don't know how I felt about Ayden. I didn't know if I liked him. I didn't know if I was gay. I didn't know if I was bisexual or what anymore. I wasn't sure about anything.

I laid in my bed and checked my phone to see what time it is.

1:37 a.m.

I stared at the ceiling and thought about Ayden and what I just did. I masturbated to a picture of him and looking at his ass.

Was that wrong? But it felt so good.

"Hmmhm" Ayden groaned in his sleep.

Did I wake him up? Did he know what I did? Would he say anything about if he knew?

He started moving around in his bed. He tossed and turned. I couldn't understand what he was mumbling in his sleep. He sat up quickly in his sleep and was breathing heavily. He looked around the room quickly and seemed to relax once he realized it was just a dream.

"Are you okay?" I asked him. I was concerned. I didn't want Ayden to feel scared. Did I?

Did I care about Ayden Grant? I don't think I have ever cared about someone.

"Just a bad dream" he mumbled, laying back down. It was late. I didn't know what I was thinking before I spoke.

"If you want, you can lay with me" I said before even thinking about what I had just said. Why would I say that to him? Did I want him in my bed? After jacking off while thinking of him.

"Um. U-Uh. I-I-I" Ayden stuttered out. Of course he would. Why would I even say something like that to him? I was so stupid sometimes.

"If you don't mind.." he trailed off not sure of my response.

"Come over then" I moved over to give him room to lie down next to me. He stood up from his bed, stretching his arms and walking over to my bed.

I couldn't help but admire his body when he was only wearing a pair of boxers that were tight around his skin. Allowing me to see everything beneath them. He looked so sexy.

I didn't even want to deny that. I knew he was hot. I didn't want to think he was hot but I knew he was.

He laid down on my bed and pulled the blanket up to his waist. We both laid there not saying anything to one another. The moonlight shone through my still open window. The wind was blowing in making it cooler than usual.

I saw Ayden shiver as a strong wind came in through the window. I put my arms over him and pulled him closer to me. I pulled the blanket higher over him to cover more of his skin and keep him warm.

"Thank you" he said. "Of course".

I was enjoying this moment. I didn't want to move from this position. I didn't want to think about anything else right now. I didn't know what I felt towards Ayden but it didn't matter.

I just wanted to hold him in my arms for the rest of the night. It felt like I had nothing to worry about. I felt calm and at peace.

Ayden's skin was so soft against mine. His hair was right below my chin. I smelled the AXE shampoo he used. It was mine and I loved the way it smelled on him. I loved that he smelled like me.

I felt soft breathing on my chest. He must have fallen asleep. Well, that was pretty quick. I wrapped my arms around Ayden tighter and closed my eyes. I wanted to enjoy this moment for as long as I could.

chapter eleven

A yden Grant

I woke up this morning pretty early around 10 o'clock. My bed was really warm today, unusually. I opened my eyes and saw Cameron.

Then everything from last night hit me. I remembered having a nightmare,waking up, then laying with Cameron in his bed and falling asleep.

Oh fuck. Why did he want me to lay with him? Did he like me?

No. Nobody likes you Ayden. You're ugly, fat, awkward, weird.

I got out of bed and took a shower and ate breakfast. Today was Saturday. Maybe I should call my mom. I hadn't talked to he in about a week. She said she would be sending me and my brother letters soon and would be allowed to call every once in awhile.

I got my phone and went outside. I was nervous to talk to my mom. Idk why, nothing has changed really.

I dialed her number and waiting for her to pick up. ring ring ring

She picked up on the third ring. "Hello" I said. "Hey, honey! How are you?"

"Mm fine you? " I asked.

We talked for about 15 minutes about different topics. I miss having my mom. I knew she needed this though. It's for the best. She needs help and this is a way for her to get it.

"Bye mom. I love you". I hung up the phone and walked back inside.

It's October 7th. 10 more days till my birthday. I wonder what I would do? I didn't have any friends to really spend it with. Or family. I didn't have anybody. I hated being lonely. But I am.

I watched some t.v. Then ate lunch. It was around 12 before Cameron woke up and came downstairs. Mr. Reese was working today and Mrs. Reese was out Christmas shopping already with some of her friends. Better early than late I suppose. And my brother Ryan was sleeping over at a friends house.

So, Cameron and I had the house to ourselves. We were going to be alone all day. Together. I was slightly nervous based on last nights events.

He walked out into the living room and greeted me with a good morning. We both watched t.v. for a little awhile in a comfortable silence.

I didn't know if I liked Cameron or not. I knew I liked boys but I don't know about him. I've only been with one person and we all know how that went.

I wonder if Cameron was even gay? How many people has he dated? Slept with?

"How many people have you slept with?" I blurted our before really thinking. He turned to me with surprise in his face.

"Uh to be honest, more than I can count." He said. Oh. He was experienced. Very experienced. Unlike me. Does he like experienced people?

He doesn't even like you Ayden. Don't get ahead of yourself.

"What was your dream about last night? Or nightmare I should say." Cameron asked me.

"Um, I had a dream about Zach.." I replied looking down.

I saw Cameron hands turn to fists and I flinched naturally.

"I'm not gonna hurt you" he reassured me.

"I'm just mad. You shouldn't be having nightmares about him. I hate what Zach did to you. I hate that he hurt you" Cameron explained.

I looked down at my lap, not wanting to look him in his face. Cameron intimidated me slightly. He never physically hurt me but he still scared me a little.

Last night you weren't scared.

But that was different. I was having a bad dream and needed comfort and he was there. Boys are confusing. Life's confusing.

"When do you turn 18?" Cameron asked me.

"10 days from today" I reasoned. Wow. I was almost 18. That's crazy to think about. Life moves so fast. It's like you blink and a year has gone by already. I would have responsibility's as an 18 year old.

I was officially an adult. I had to get a job to support myself. I had to pay taxes, bills, get a place to live, go to college, so many things to do.

"What do you wanna do for it?" He asked me. What did I want to do?

"Um, I'm not sure" I said honestly.

"Well think about. You only turn eighteen once so you gotta make it worth it." he told me.

What do you usually do on a birthday? I've never really done anything special. Go out to dinner have cake and open gifts. Just something casual.

We spent the rest of the day just hanging out. Nothing special happened between Cameron and I.

The school week went by with nothing bad happening to me. It was like people had forgotten about the whole picture that I sent. It's crazy how something can be such a big deal and feel like it's ruining your life and then the next week it's like nothing ever happened. But that was high school.

I was busy with school work and Cameron was usually out with his friends I guess because he wasn't at home after school. We hadn't really talked much since Saturday. It felt like nothing had happened between us.

Maybe it was just a one time thing and I'm over analyzing things. Would he even consider me a friend? He was nice to me and it seemed like he cared about me.

I missed him. I wanted to talk to Cameron and spend time with him. I shouldn't feel this way but I can't help myself. I think I was started to get feelings for Cameron.

"I liked Cameron" I said to myself.

I didn't think those words would ever come out of my mouth but they did.

I liked Cameron Reese.

Chapter Twelve

Ayden Grant

Today was the day I was finally an adult. I was eighteen years old. I still felt the same as before. I didn't have any plans but Mr. Reese and Mrs. Reese wanted to go out to dinner. Which I was thankful for.

We were on our way to the Cheesecake Factory. I had never been there before but I heard their food was good.

"Happy birthday Ayden" Cameron said.

"Thank you" I said. Today was Friday so we waited till around 5 o'clock for my brother to get home from school so we could all go. I was really hungry since I hadn't eaten all day. School food was gross so I didn't usually eat at lunch.

The restaurant wasn't that far away. We got there within 10 minutes. We had to wait a few minutes before being seated and ordering our food.

I ordered Fettuccini Alfredo. I loved Italian food. I'm not sure I've ever had it before but it sounded delicious.

Our food came quickly and we all started eating. It was some of the best food I'd ever had in my life.

"Mmm" I didn't even realize I made that noise when I took the first bite until I saw Cameron looking at me.

He had this unrecognizable look in his eyes. He put his hand on my thigh and just stared at me.

I went back to eating my food and tried not to think about his hand on my leg. He kept it there the whole time we were eating. It made me feel anxious.

We had dessert and went home.

"We got you a few things Ayden" Mrs. Reese announced in the car.

"Thank you. I appreciate it but you guys didn't really have to get me anything" I told her.

"I know honey but we wanted too" she told me.

I had 2 gifts from them. And one other with no name on it. I opened the first gift it was 20$. Money was always a good gift. You can never go wrong with it tbh.

The second gift was a new phone. I really needed a new one because my first one was so cracked and an iPhone 5s but I just didn't have money to buy a new one.

"Wow. Thank you so much" I was really grateful for everything they given me. Not just presents but a place to live and everything.

I still had one gift left. "That one is from me" Cameron said. I looked at him with surprise.

I opened the the present and saw that it was a necklace shaped like a heart. It had the words: "you're stronger than you think you are" engraved into it.

I smiled. I loved the necklace so much. "Thank you. I love it" I told Cameron.

"I thought you would" he said.

"Help me put it on?" I asked.

He took the necklace from my hands and put it on for me. I picked it up and read the words over again. I smiled at the thought that Cameron took time to get me a gift for my birthday.

We hung out in the living room, just talking about random topics while I set up my new phone. It was 10:00 o'clock before everyone went to sleep or to their own rooms.

Cameron and I went upstairs and kept talking about whatever came to our minds. "How was your eighteenth birthday" he asked.

"It was really good" I said genuinely. Today was actually pretty good.

"I'm glad you had a good day". Then I remembered Cameron's hand on my thing throughout the whole dinner. I didn't question it then because we were in front of other people and I didn't want to make it awkward at dinner.

"Um, why did you. You know. Uh. Putyourhandonmythighatdinner" I blurted our quickly. He laughed and shook his head "Can you repeat that? A little slower this time."

"Why did you put your hand on my thigh during dinner?" I asked again this time slower so he could understand what I was saying.

"Just claiming what's mine" he said casually, like it was the most normal thing in the world to say.

I started at him with my mouth open, not even knowing what to say.

Just claiming what's mine.

I didn't even know what to say to that. What does that even mean? Does this mean Cameron likes me? He wants to be with me?

"What?" I asked, realizing I should probably say something.

He stood up and walked over to me. He looked down at me "You heard what I said". I did but I didn't know what to even think of that.

"I like you Ayden".

Chapter Thirteen

Cameron Reese

"I like you Ayden" the words left my mouth before I even thought of what I was saying.

I didn't know how I felt towards Ayden till this week. He was a guy. I was a guy. Two guys in a relationship is wrong?

I thought.

I didn't know if I was straight or gay. I wanted to be straight but I knew deep down I wasn't. I just didn't want to admit it.

I thought.

I felt like once I said the words out loud that it made them true. I didn't want to be gay. I wanted to be normal. Gay isn't normal. Gay is wrong. Straight is right. But Ayden's gay. He's not wrong. Is he?

I thought.

Every day this week, after school I would find some girl to hook up with. I was desperate to try and get rid of my "feelings" I had seemed to catch for Ayden. I didn't want to like him. But I did.

I fucked 4 girls. One on Monday. Tuesday. Wednesday. Thursday. No one today. Today was Friday. Ayden's birthday. I didn't want to be with some hoe. I wanted to be with him.

Out of the four girls I had fucked none of them felt good. It felt wrong. I could barley get hard and I didn't even want to have sex with any of them but I did. Each time I thought of Ayden. I couldn't help myself. I would close my eyes and imagine it was him moaning and not some girl.

The only reason I fucked those girls was because I wanted to be normal. I wanted to be straight. I realize now that I'm not straight. I'm gay.

I like boys even though I had never been with one. I knew I liked boys now or one boy. Ayden.

I liked Ayden Grant. And he was a boy.

I told him I was claiming what's mine. I wanted him to be mine. I wanted him now. I walked over to him. He was sitting on his bed looking up at me. He looked so innocent and pure. That turned me on even more.

I was a little horny. I hadn't had sex today. I wanted to but I didn't. My only opinion right now was Ayden. I wanted to fuck him. Right now.

I sat down on his bed and motioned for him to sit on my lap. He looked at me for a second before moving over.

I stared at him and said "I want to make you feel good". Which is true. I did want him to feel good.

I took off his shirt and kissed his neck and collarbone. I left love bites all over his chest and collarbone area. I didn't want anyone else to have Ayden. I was selfish. I wanted him for myself. I didn't want any other guy to have him. This is my way of ensuring that he didn't have anyone else.

Ayden didn't stop me, he just allowed me to do what I pleased. I flipped us over so I was on top of him and he was laying down. I gave him kisses all the way from his neck, to his chest, to his waist, and to his hips until I reached his pants.

I unbuttoned his pants and pulled them off. I took of my own shirt as well so he wouldn't be the only one without clothes on.

"Um, what are you doing?" Ayden asked looking unsure.

"Giving you a blowjob" I said casually. He stared at me with wide eyes and his mouth open. The things I could put in there.

"Is that okay?" I asked. He stared at me for a minute and then nodded. I continued to pull off his boxers and threw them to the side. He was hot. Ayden was sexy.

I opened my mouth and wrapped my lips around his cock and began sucking it. I heard him moan instantly.

"Oh fuck" he muttered. I knew he was feeling good by the was his eyes were closed tightly and the noises coming from his mouth.

I kept doing this until I knew he would come soon. I wanted to save that for later. He looked up to me and said "why'd you stop?"

"Can't cum just yet" I told him. He sat up and looked at me.

"What are you doing?" I asked. "I want to return the favor."

"You don't have too. Just let me make you feel good, Ayden" I said. He smiled at me and I told him to lay back down on his stomach this time.

Ayden had a cute ass. It was small yet still cute. It looked like a girls one but better. I loved it.

I bent down and held his butt with my hands. I slipped my tongue between them and started moving it circularly around his hole. I moved it in and out of his ass.

"Mmm" Ayden was moaning loud. Too loud. My parents were going to hear him if he wasn't quieter. But I knew he felt good. I wanted him to feel good tonight.

"Be quieter, if you don't want my parents walking in" I told him. "Mm can't, feels to good" he murmured.

I went back to eating out his ass and I added one finger in. His hole was so tight. I didn't expect that. But it was so hot to me.

"It hurts" Ayden whined. "It'll feel better soon" I told him.

"Do the other thing with your tongue, that felt better".

I laughed and kept fucking him with my finger. I added two more to which Ayden was not happy with. I knew it hurt him now but he would feel better soon.

He groaned in pain as I added a third finger into his already extremely tight hole.

I leaned over him and whispered in his ear "I'm gonna take care of you and make you feel so good baby."

He nodded and I got up to grab some lube because my dick was not gonna go in dry. I came back and spread it over his hole and on my dick. I told Ayden to flip back over so I could see his face while I fucked him and made him feel good.

"You ready?" I asked. He bit his lip and looked at me with worry. He nodded hesitantly. Him biting his lip only turned me on more. I slid my dick into his hole slowly, trying my best to not hurt him. He was so fucking tight though. I wasn't even sure my dick would fit all the way.

His face scrunched up in pain and I felt bad. He was groaning in pain. I kept fucking him until his groans turned into moans. I leaned in asked "How are you feeling, baby?"

"Great daddy" he said with his eyes still closed.

Great daddy.

Those words turned me on so much. I started fucking him even harder and faster than before. My thrusts were getting sloppier but I didn't care. I was about to cum. I kept going until I came in Ayden's ass.

"Oh fuck yeah" he moaned. I grabbed his dick and started stroking him until he came on my hand.

I went to the bathroom and came back with a towel. I cleaned off my hand and around his ass where some of my cum had leaked out. I threw the towel on the floor and laid next to Ayden.

His eyes were closed and I just stared at him. He was so beautiful. His face was perfect, his hair, his body. He was perfect.

"That felt amazing" he said bringing me out of my thoughts.

"Yes it did" I agreed. It was the first time I had sex with a guy and it was amazing. It was the best sex I've ever had.

I grabbed his chest and pulled him closer to me. I pulled his blanket over us and held him for the rest of the night. I fell asleep with him in my arms and it felt amazing.

Chapter Fourteen

Ayden Grant

"Cameron. Cameron. Cameron" I repeated his name until he woke up.

"My butt hurts" I frowned. He smirked and said "Well yeah, you had a dick in there last night".

I blushed and turned away at the thought of last night. It felt amazing. I didn't even know your body could feel that amount of pleasure from another human being. I loved it. Well most of it.

"You're cute when you blush" Cameron said only making my face redder. We were still laying in the same position from last night. I didn't know what time it was but the sun wasn't up yet. "What time is it?" I asked.

"6:22" he said. "It's too early, go back to sleep."

"I can't. I'm in pain. You're the one who caused it, so you should fix it" I told him.

"Oh, should I now?" I could hear the smirk in his voice. "Yes, you should."

"Well, I'm afraid there's nothing that can really help you" Cameron said. "Maybe taking a bath" he suggested.

I got out of bed to go to the bathroom and take a bath, like he suggested. "Where are you going?" He whined.

"To take a bath." "And leave me, by myself?" He asked.

"Come join if you want, then" I said. I don't know where I got this sudden confidence from. A minute ago I was blushing because he called me cute and now I was telling him to take a bath with me. Naked.

Cameron stood up and followed behind me into the bathroom. He closed the door and locked it behind himself. I looked at myself in the mirror and saw all the hickeys on my chest. "Why'd you do that?" I asked him. "Marking what's mine." He replied simply. I blushed again at his words. He was so blunt sometimes but I liked that about him.

He walked over to the bath and turned the facet on. I sat down in the tub as the water started to fill. I loved baths. They were so relaxing. I loved the feeling of the warm water against my skin. I felt Cameron sit behind me and wrap his arms around my chest and put his head on my shoulder.

We had sex last night. I never had sex before. I hadn't ever gotten that far with a guy before. "I'm a virgin. Or was one" I said quickly. "You are?" Cameron asked.

"Yeah, I've never gotten that far with a guy before." I explained to him.

"So, I was your first?" He said more to himself than me. Wow. I feel special now." He laughed.

"That's why you were so tight, huh?" He said. "Yeah I guess so."

I stayed in the bath for about an hour, I got out when the water was cold. Cameron followed me, of course. I went back to our room and got dressed in sweatpants and t shirt.

I laid back down in my bed and closed my eyes. I was still tired however, my butt did feel better.

Does Cameron like me? What are we? We had sex last night.

"Cameron, can I ask you a question?"

"Technically, you just asked me a question but yeah go ahead." He said.

"What are we?" I asked genuinely curious.

"Well, last night, you called me daddy." He replied. "I'm your daddy Ayden."

Somebody has a daddy kink.

I laughed at him. "Seriously?" I asked. "I like you Ayden. I wanna be with you."

He liked me?! He wanted to be with me?!

"Are you serious? You wanna be with me?" I asked in shock.

"Yes, I do."

"Well, I like you too, Cameron." I don't know when I realized I liked him, I just knew I did.

"I wanna be able to call you mine. I don't want anybody else to have you. I want you all for myself." He told me.

I smiled at him "I want that too."

We laid in bed and talked. About whatever came to our minds. Life was good. I was happy. I hadn't felt that in a long time. I felt like I belonged.

I was grateful for that.

Chapter Fifteen

Ayden Grant

Monday. Ugh. I hate Monday's. For many reasons. You have to wake up early to go to school. It's the furthest day from Friday. And they just suck.

I slept in late today, because that's my luck. I got dressed quickly and grabbed my backpack while running out the door. I didn't want to be late to school today. It brought attention to myself. Unwanted attention. I didn't like being the spotlight of the room. It made me feel uncomfortable.

I walked fast to school to get there on time. Luckily I wasn't late and made it to my first period just as the bell was ringing.

Cameron wasn't going to school today to go look at colleges and universities. I didn't know what college I wanted to go to yet. I should probably figure that out soon though.

My day wasn't great but it wasn't bad either. It was kinda boring.

Ding

From: Cameron

Hey, boo. I just got finished looking at colleges. I'm gonna go out with my friends for awhile. I'll see you soon.

I smiled at my phone as I read his message. He was so sweet.

To: Cameron

Okay, I'll see you at home.

My day was almost over. I had two periods left. I couldn't focus on anything today. I wasn't thinking about anything in particular. My mind was scattered today for some reason.

I got home and cooked a frozen pizza because I was starving. I usually didn't eat at school, so I was always hungry when I got home. The pizza was actually good considering it was a frozen Walmart brand pizza.

"Hey honey, we need to have a little talk" Stacey (Mrs. Reese) said to me.

"Uh okay, what about?" I asked her.

"Something important, I wanna wait for Sean (Mr. Reese) to get home though. He should be here within an hour or so. He thought he could get out a little early today." She explained.

"Well I'll be upstairs, until he gets here then." I said. She smiled at me with a sad look in her eyes. What could they wanna talk about? Where they gonna ask me to move out since I was eighteen now? Did I do something wrong?

My mind was filled with so many ideas about what they could possibly wanna talk about with me. Did they find out about me and Cameron? I hadn't even thought about that. If they found we were dating they would probably kick me out. They wouldn't want their son and his boyfriend sleeping together in the same room I assumed.

Knock knock

I quickly jumped up to see who was at the door. It was Sean. "Hey, kid. Wanna come downstairs, so we can talk?" He asked.

"Yeah" I agreed and followed him down the stairs and into the living room. Stacey was already sitting on the sofa and Sean took a seat next to her. I sat across from them and waited for them to tell me what they wanted too.

I was nervous. Actually I was very nervous. I was scared of what they were going to say to me.

"Well Ayden, there's no easy way to say this to someone. Especially a kid. Your mother was given a drug by someone from outside of the rehab center. They aren't sure who but assuming it was someone she knew well. And the drug was heroin, which you know she struggled with addiction for many years. The reason she's there and you and Ryan are here. So, um, she overdosed on heroin last night. They called an ambulance and she was hospitalized but by the time they found her body she had stopped breathing and her organs had began to shut down. She was pronounced dead at the hospital."

I felt numb. No. She wasn't dead. She couldn't be dead. She was my mom. Moms don't die. They don't leave their kids.

"We're here for you, if you need anything. If you wanna talk to somebody. Anything Ayden. We love you just as much as our son." Mrs. Reese pulled me into a hug and held me tight. I didn't hug her back. I just sat there. I didn't know what to do. I didn't know what to say.

"I'm gonna go think." I mumbled and went to go back upstairs. I walked over to my bed and sat down.

She wasn't gone. She still here. She's not dead. She wouldn't leave us. She loved me. When you love someone, you don't leave them.

What's the purpose in living? How can I even live without my mom? She's the only person I had. How could she leave so unexpected? She was there to get help. But she didn't. She died there.

No she didn't die there. She was alive.

I grabbed my phone and called her.

ring ring ring ring the number you have called is not available at this time please leave a message after the beep.

"Hey, mom. You're probably busy right now. Whenever you can call me back. I just wanna talk to you. I miss you so much. I love you mom, goodbye."

She was still here. She was just busy. Yeah, she was just busy I told myself.

Call log:

Mom: 20 outgoing calls within last hour.

ring ring ring ring the number you have called is not available at this time please leave a message after the beep.

"Hey mom. Sorry to call you so much but I just really need to talk to you. It's very important. Call me back as soon as you can. I love you, goodbye."

It's been 3 hours. She still hasn't called back or texted. Cameron walked into the bedroom frantically and saw me. He walked over to me and asked "Are you okay?" He looked sad and concerned. I don't know why, nothing had happened. I was perfectly fine.

"I'm fine. Nothing has happened." I told him truthfully. He gave me a confused look, not saying anything for a minute and then looking down. "You sure?" He asked again.

"Yeah, I'm great." I replied. Maybe I should try again. It was currently 8 o'clock so she shouldn't be busy now.

"Give me a second, I gotta call someone" I told him. I picked up my phone, dialing my moms number once again.

ring ring ring ring the number you have called is not available at this time please leave a message after the beep.

"Hey, mom. Sorry for calling so much. I just wanna talk to you. I thought you wouldn't be busy now but I guess you are. Give me call when you're free. I love you. Bye." I ended the call once again. I felt like a broken record player. I had pretty much said the same thing everytime I called her and it went straight to voicemail.

"Um, I'm gonna go downstairs for a bit. I'll be back up soon" Cameron said looking confused and a little sad. He walked out of the room and I laid back down in bed deciding to go to sleep and try talking to my mom tomorrow.

Chapter Sixteen

Cameron Reese

I heard the news from my parents that Ayden's mom had died in the hospital. As soon as they told me I ran to our room to check on him. I was worried about him. He was sitting on his bed not doing anything. Just laying there. He didn't look sad or happy. He didn't have any emotion on his face.

I asked him how he was to which he responded great. He wasn't upset. He wasn't hurt. He wasn't crying. It was like nothing had happened. He made a phone call to someone I assumed one of his friends then I heard him say I love you mom.

That's when I knew, that Ayden was in denial. He thought his mom was still living. That's why he wasn't upset. That's why he wasn't crying. That's why he was acting normal.

I went downstairs to tell my parents. They were down there telling Ryan, Ayden's younger brother, the same news. My mom was holding him as he cried.

"Dad, can I talk to you for a minute?" I asked. We walked out of the living room and into the kitchen for more privacy.

"He's in denial. He doesn't think his mom is dead. He called her cell phone." I told my dad everything Ayden had done.

"Yeah, that's expected when you lose a loved one, for them to be in denial. They don't want to believe it's true." He explained to me.

"What do I do?" I asked him.

"You can't do anything. He has to be the one to realize she's gone. The only thing you can do is be there for him, comfort him. That's all you can do. You can't take away their pain." My dad told me.

"Okay." I nodded my head and went back upstairs to see Ayden in the same position as when I left.

I walked over to his bed and sat down next to him. "Maybe I should call, just one last time. She's just busy right now. It's close to the holidays." He was reasoning with himself.

I couldn't let him keep calling her and getting no answer. He would never get to hear her voice again. She would never answer his phone call again. It was impossible. She was gone. I couldn't let him think that he was going to get some kind of answer.

"Ayden. Your moms gone. She's not coming back. She is dead. She won't answer the phone, no matter how many times you call or leave voicemails" I told him. I had too.

"Why would you say that?" He looked up at me with tears in his eyes. It felt like someone had ripped my heart out of my body. I hated seeing him sad. I couldn't stand to watch him be upset and I had no control over it. I couldn't make him feel better. I just had to watch him go through the pain of losing someone.

Ayden got off his bed and stood in front of me. He was slightly taller than me when I was sitting and he was standing.

"I hate you!" He said to me. He took off his necklace that I had given him and threw it on the ground. "I hate you so much! You're the worst person in the world!" He yelled at me. He walked over to my bed and started throwing off all the pillows and blankets from it onto the floor.

"You're so mean to me. You hurt me. I hate you." He started grabbing things off my dresser and throwing them at me.

I knew he didn't mean those words. I knew he didn't hate me. But it still hurt a lot to hear those words coming from his mouth. I walked over to him and stopped him before he could grab anything expensive or breakable. I hugged him even though he tried to push me away from him.

He was crying so hard he could barley talk. "G-g-get-t-t of-f-f of me-e-e" he said. I wouldn't let him go though. I held him tighter in my arms. He turned around so he was facing me and started punching me in an attempt to make me let go of him. His punches were weak though and they failed to work on me.

"Ayden. Calm down. Please." I begged him.

He cried in my arms harder and kept saying "She's gone. She's gone. She's gone."

I felt so useless at this moment. Nothing I could do would make Ayden feel better. He was grieving with the pain. I felt like I had been holding him forever until he had stopped crying and was just standing there with me.

"Let's lay down." I said to him. He didn't respond. I let go of him to pick up my pillows and put them back on my bed. I grabbed the blankets and placed them on there too.

I took off my jeans and shirt to be more comfortable. I asked Ayden if he wanted to change his clothes and all I got was a nod. I took off his shirt and pants. I walked back over to my bed and laid down. He soon came over and joined me.

I pulled the blanket over us and hugged him. He didn't respond. He didn't say anything, move, or even look at me. He laid there looking up at the ceiling.

"You should get some rest." I told him. Ayden nodded and closed his eyes. I held him until I fell asleep. I hoped to wake up and this all be some horrible nightmare. But this wasn't a nightmare. This was reality.

Chapter Seventeen

Ayden Grant

She was really gone. Why couldn't it have been me? Why did it have to be her? I should be the one who's gone. I'm useless. I don't deserve to live. But she does.

I stayed home from school for the rest of the week. It had been two days since mom passed away. Her funeral was today. I didn't think I was ready for it.

I was dressed up in a black suit, like everyone else. Wearing black made funerals even sadder. But I guess that's the point. Funerals aren't supposed to be happy, they're supposed to be sad.

I didn't let myself cry during the funeral. I hadn't stopped crying for the past two days. I didn't want to cry anymore. I don't even think I could make tears anymore.

After the funeral we went out to lunch and then came home. The food was okay. I don't really remember how it tasted.

"Ayden," Cameron called my name. We hadn't talked much since Monday night. The night I went crazy and started throwing stuff. I'm so fucked up. I fucking hate myself so much.

"What do you want?!" I snapped at him. I didn't mean to. I was angry all of a sudden. I wasn't really sure where it came from.

Cameron looked at me with shock evident on his face "Do you want me to put on the necklace I gave you?" He asked shyly. I didn't think Cameroon would ever be shy.

"I don't want your stupid necklace! Okay?! I don't even like you. I hate you! So leave me alone!" I yelled at him.

I couldn't tell what he was feeling based on his facial expressions. He didn't look happy though. It was a mixture of anger and sadness.

Cameron walked over to me and grabbed my jaw making me look up at him. "You don't hate me." He said.

"I actually do." I replied. Did I hate him? Why would I hate him? He hasn't done anything wrong to me? Has he? I was putting all my anger on to him for no reason.

"No you don't. You would never hate me. Ever." Cameron told me. He was still holding my jaw. "Let go of me!" I told him. I didn't want to be near him.

"No. Not until you admit you don't hate me."

"Well, too bad for you. Because I do hate you. I hate you so much." I told him. I didn't mean those words. Why was I saying this to him?

"What's your problem?!" I yelled at him. He had pushed me against the wall. Rather violently, I might add. "Showing you." He kissed my neck. "That you don't." He whispered in my ear. "Hate me." He said looking into my eyes.

He pulled off my shirt and let his hands roam all over my chest. "It's not working." I said.

"Oh, baby. I haven't even started yet." He smiled up at me. More like a smirk. Like he knew something I didn't. He bent down and grabbed my legs. He walked over to his bed and put me down.

"I wanna fuck you." He said bluntly. "But more importantly, I wanna make love to you. I wanna show you what love feels like. Make you feel so good. Show you that you don't hate me at all." Cameron said while kissing my chest.

My breathing got heavier. His words impacted me. And his kisses. I should just apologize to him. Tell him that I didn't hate him. I didn't mean those words I had said a few moments ago. I was stubborn though. Very stubborn. I didn't want to admit I was wrong.

Cameron pulled off my pants and underwear. He grabbed my dick and started stroking it slowly. It felt amazing but I wouldn't let him know that. I couldn't.

He stared into my eyes and asked "You feel good?" I didn't answer him. He raised an eyebrow at me and smirked once again.

He rubbed his fingers against my hole. I let out a moan unconsciously. I didn't mean to. It just slipped out.

Cameron smiled at me. He leaned down and whispered in my ear "Say the word and you could be in a whole other world of pleasure right now."

"No."

"Okay, then have it your way." He said. Cameron sat up and walked over to his t.v. turning it on. He grabbed his controller and head set, then sat on the edge of the bed.

"Wha-" he left me like this. As soon I was getting horny, he left me.

He turned around and looked at me "You hate me. Why would you want me to make you feel good?"

"Uh-h I-I" I stuttered out. He had a point but I don't hate him.

"I don't hate you." I finally said. Cameron smiled at me and put his game controller up.

"So, you don't hate me?" He asked.

"No, I don't. I didn't mean that" I told him. I really didn't. I don't know why I had said it.

Cameron kissed my whole chest making his way down to my lower area. He started sucking my cock. It was one of the best feelings I ever experienced. I didn't want it to end. I didn't even try to control my moans this time.

As he was sucking my dick, he put his fingers back inside my hole. It felt amazing as well.

"You're still tight."

"I haven't been with anyone else," I told him.

"Good. Because you're mine. Only mine." Cameron said. I smiled at his words. I liked Cameron. I wanted to be his. We never really talked about what we were.

"Do you want my cock inside of you?"

"Yes, please." moaned out.

"Yes, please what?" He asked.

"I don't know what?" I asked him. What did he want me to say?

"Oh, you know," he leaned down so his lips were brushing my ear as he spoke "daddy."

My whole body got chills from his voice. "Please, daddy?" I asked.

Cameron smilies triumphantly. He lined his cock up with my assole. It burned slightly but I knew it would feel better in a few moments. He fucked me so hard. I had a layer of sweat over my body as did he.

"I want you to ride me."

I was nervous. I had never done that before. What if I wasn't good? What if I messed up?

We switched positions, Cameron was now under me as I sat on his lap. I was leaning back on my knees as I grabbed his dick.

I lined it up to my hole and slowly sat down on it. I was the one in control now. I was riding him, then I saw Cameron's face. He was looking at me with this emotion.

I didn't even know how to describe it. He looked like he was at a lost for words but in a good way. He looked like he was daydreaming almost. A look of happiness.

"Daddy, you make me feel so good." I decided to tease him to see his reaction.

The day dream state he was in immediately went away as he looked up at me.

He grabbed my hips and looked into my eyes as he smirked, "Oh yea, baby? Guess what? You're gonna make me cum." He answered his own question.

I felt Cameron cum in my ass. It was an odd feeling but I liked it. He used his hand to pleasure me until I released onto his chest. I got off of him and laid down next to him.

He walked out of the room and came back with a towel. He cleaned my butt and then wiped off his chest. He threw the towel onto his dirty clothes pile.

We laid down in his bed and both went to sleep. I guess having sex makes you tired. Makes sense.

I was sleeping until around 3 o'clock in the morning. I sat up quickly in bed. My first thought was my mom.

Mom.

She was gone and here I was having sex. I shouldn't be having sex. No it wasn't right. I felt a tear fall down my face. What the fuck is wrong with me? Why am I such a fuck up?

Chapter Eighteen

Ayden Grant

To whom it may concern, I am leaving this note with my last words.

I hate myself. I hate being alive. I have kept this in as I am too coward to seek help. Which has lead me to this.

My life has no meaning at this point in time. I fuck up everything and please excuse my language this time but I am a fuck up. I able to do nothing right. Everything I do I mess up some how. I used to believe that everything happened for a reason. I used to believe in life.

There is no point in me living any longer. I am a waste of oxygen. I have no purpose on this earth. The pain has become too much to bare. I am not strong enough to conceal my wounds any longer. Which is why I am doing this.

This was never your fault, to whoever is reading this. This is my choice. My decision. My fault. I don't blame anyone else but myself for the way I am and what this has come too. Do not blame yourselves for my actions.

Ryan, I love you. You are the best brother I've ever had. Please be strong. Do not be like me. I wish you the best. You will do amazing things with your life. You will be somebody.

Mr. and Mrs. Reese, you have given me more than I could ever ask for. You have blessed me and my brother with a home, food, clothes and so much more. But most importantly you've given me love. The parental love that every person needs. The unbreakable, everlasting bond between two human beings. You have treated me as if I was one of your own. For that I can not thank you enough.

Cameron, you have seen me at my worst. More than enough times. You didn't leave me or laugh at me. Instead, you were there for me. You comforted me when no one else would. We laughed together, loved, and lived. I can honestly say that you've changed my life. When I'm with you my problems temporarily go away.

But that's the issue. Temporary isn't enough. I need more than that. I don't want to be suffering in pain any longer. Please forgive my actions of taking my own life. I wish you all the best. With best regards, Ayden Grant.

I signed my name at the bottom of my paper. This was it. These were going to be my last words. The last words that anyone would hear of me. I walked into my room and laid the paper on Cameron's bed. I wanted him to be the first to read my suicide note.

I walked outside for about 10 minutes until I reached the bus stop. The wait wasn't long before the city bus pulled in. A few people got off, as I got on. I walked to the back of the back of the bus and sat in the last row of the seats. The bus soon reached its next stop.

The Golden Gate Bridge

I walked down the walkway to the bridge. People were passing by not giving a second glance towards me. They didn't know what I was about to do. No one did.

No one cares.

I ran forward using both of my hands I launched myself off the railing. My last thought:

I don't wanna die.

chapter nineteen

Cameron Reese

The words didn't process through my mind. It was my 3rd time reading the letter before I realized I was wasting time.

I had no idea where he was. I had no idea where to look for him.

"Suicide off Golden Gate Bridge. The body of a young male recently found floating on top of the water. The male has not yet been identified. If you have any information please contact us immediately-"

No. No. No.

This isn't real life. It's not Ayden. No way.

I ran as quickly as I could to the bridge. There were cop cars and ambulances surrounding the area. It felt like my whole world slowed down. Everything went silent.

I fell to my knees and cried. I cried. That's all I could do at the moment. I finally looked up to see his body.

It was Ayden's body. He looked almost unrecognizable. He wasn't moving. This wasn't it. He couldn't be dead. There was no way. I never got to tell him that I loved him.

"You can't be here, sir," one of the officers addressed me.

"He's my boyfriend."

"Sir, he has passed away. The impact of the water killed him instantly. Falling from that height is like hitting concrete. I'm sorry for your loss."

It felt like I had been stabbed in the chest with a knife. Then, that person took that knife and twisted it deepening the wound further.

I broke at that moment. I felt my body shut down. He's gone. I wasn't quick enough to save him. I wasn't strong enough for him. I wasn't there for him.

I grabbed Ayden's hand. "I love you," I whispered to him as tears fell down my cheeks.

It was the slightest sensation. The tiniest movement but I felt it. His hand had squeezed my own.

"He's alive! He's still alive!" Everyone looked at me like I had lost my mind. "He squeezed my hand. I felt it. Hurry! He needs medical attention now!" I yelled out.

The EMT quickly rushed over to us. Ayden was put in the ambulance as I sat next to him holding his hand the whole way there.

It felt like the longest car ride of my life. Every second mattered now more than ever.

We got to the hospital and he was rushed inside. They took him back to one of the emergency rooms.

I paced back in forth in the waiting room, impatiently waiting for results.

"Cameron." A nurse called my name. I quickly rushed over to her.

"Ayden's on breathing tubes for oxygen, and has multiple iv's. His bones in his lower back are shattered. He needs more blood than the hospital currently has. He's alive but barley. That kid is a miracle." The nurse explained to me.

I broke out into the biggest smile. My Ayden was alive. He was in a bad condition but he was alive.

"Would you be willing to donate blood for him?" The nurse continued.

"Yes. Of course, whatever he needs." I told her. I would give Ayden anything he needed.

She took me back to a room and drew blood out of my arm. After she finished she led me to his room.

"He's in critical condition right now. Please be very careful around him." She told me.

I nodded my head and walked in. He had so many tubes and wires connected to his body. I sat down on the chair next to the bed. I grabbed his hand.

"Ayden. You are the love of my life. You have changed me. I don't know where I would be without you right now. You are the best thing that has ever happened to me. I truly love you more than words Ayden Grant."

I felt his hand squeeze mine ever so slightly. "We're gonna get through this together. I can promise you that."

Chapter Twenty

Ayden Grant

"Daddy!" I held out my arms as my two son ran into my arms. Cameron and I adopted twins after we got married. They were 5 years old today.

Time flew by. It feels like just yesterday I was feeding them a bottle and now they were going to start school this year.

"Happy birthday Grayson and Ethan!"

"I five years old today" Grayson said holding up five fingers.

"Me too!" Ethan said.

"I know. You're both getting so big." I couldn't believe they were already five years old. "Let's go wake up papa."

They both ran into the bedroom to wake up Cameron. As I walked in they were both jumping on the bed yelling "Papa! Get up."

"I five years old now." "Me too Papa."

"Happy birthday!" Cameron told them. I smiled at the scene in front of me. My husband and my two kids. Life felt perfect.

"Good morning." He said to me.

Cameron walked over to me and pulled me into a hug. "You know what else today is?" He asked me.

I smiled sadly, "Suicide prevention day."

He squeezed my hand, "I love you."

"I love you more than you'll ever know Ayden."

Life is the greatest gift we've ever been given.

www.ingramcontent.com/pod-product-compliance
Lightning Source LLC
Chambersburg PA
CBHW071008080526
44587CB00015B/2385